Cocktails & Coloring

new seasons®
a division of Publications International, Ltd.

Let's get social!

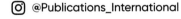 @Publications_International

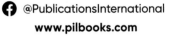 @PublicationsInternational

www.pilbooks.com

gin & tonic

2 oz GIN
4 oz TONIC WATER
LIME WEDGE

Fill old fashioned glass with ice; pour gin over ice. Stir in tonic water. Garnish with lime wedge.

Makes 1 serving

Martini

2 ounces vodka or gin

½ ounce dry vermouth

Fill cocktail shaker half full with ice; add gin and vermouth. Stir or shake until blended; strain into cocktail glass.

Makes 1 serving

MOSCOW MULE

½ **LIME, cut into 2 wedges**

1½ **ounces** VODKA

4 to 6 ounces chilled GINGER BEER

Lime slices and fresh MINT **sprigs**

 Fill copper mug half full with ice; squeeze lime juice over ice and drop wedges into mug. Pour vodka over ice; top with ginger beer. Garnish with lime slices and mint.

Cranberry Caipirinha

2 lime wedges

1 orange wedge

12 fresh cranberries

2 tablespoons packed brown sugar

2 ounces cachaça

1 ounce cranberry juice

Lime slice

Muddle lime wedges, orange wedge, cranberries and brown sugar in mixing glass or cocktail shaker. Add cachaça, cranberry juice and ice; shake until blended. Strain into ice-filled old fashioned glass; garnish with lime slice.

Makes 1 serving

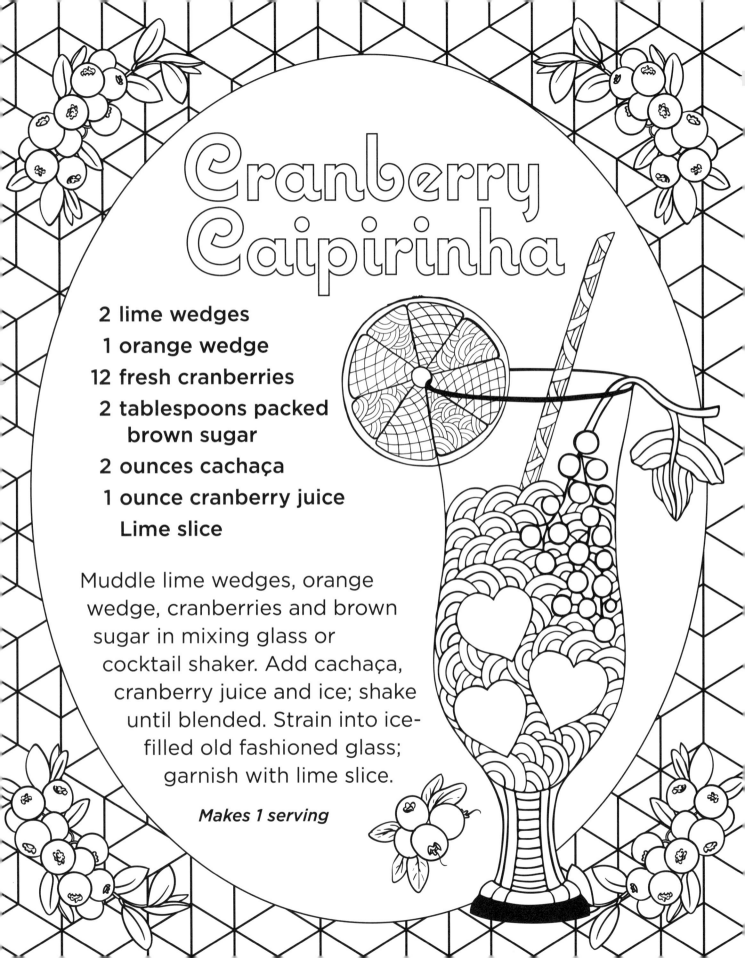

tequila sunrise

2 ounces tequila

6 ounces orange juice

1 tablespoon grenadine

Strawberry or lime slice

Place 4 ice cubes in tall glass. Pour tequila and orange juice over ice; do not stir. Pour in grenadine; let sink to bottom of glass. (Do not stir.) Garnish with strawberry slice.

Makes 1 serving

Daiquiri

MAKES 1 SERVING

1½ OUNCES LIGHT RUM

¾ OUNCE LIME JUICE

¼ OUNCE SIMPLE SYRUP

LIME WEDGE

Fill cocktail shaker half full with ice; add rum, lime juice and simple syrup. Shake until blended; strain into cocktail glass. Garnish with lime wedge.

SIMPLE SYRUP: Combine 1 cup water and 1 cup sugar in small saucepan. Cook over medium heat just until sugar is dissolved, stirring frequently. Cool to room temperature; store syrup in glass jar in refrigerator.

ROSÉ SANGRIA

MAKES 8 SERVINGS

1 cup orange juice
½ cup sugar
2 bottles rosé wine
(750ml each)

¼ cup lime or lemon juice
1 orange, thinly sliced
1 lime, thinly sliced
16 to 20 ice cubes

1. Combine orange juice and sugar in small saucepan; cook over medium heat just until sugar is dissolved, stirring occasionally. Pour into large pitcher. Add wine, lime juice and orange and lemon slices; cover and refrigerate 2 hours for flavors to blend.

2. Serve sangria in ice-filled glasses.

FROZEN MUDSLIDE

1 cup vanilla ice cream

1 ounce vodka

1 ounce coffee liqueur

1 ounce Irish cream liqueur

1 to 2 tablespoons cream (optional)

Chocolate syrup (optional)

Whipped cream

1. Combine ice cream, vodka, coffee liqueur and Irish cream liqueur in blender; blend until smooth. Add cream, if desired, to reach desired consistency.

2. Hold serving glass at an angle; gently squeeze chocolate syrup onto side of glass while turning glass. Or squeeze syrup in vertical squiggles up and down side of glass.

3. Pour drink into prepared glass; garnish with whipped cream.

Makes 1 serving

Mojito

MAKES 1 SERVING

4 fresh mint leaves, plus additional sprigs for garnish

1 ounce lime juice

1 teaspoon superfine sugar or powdered sugar

1½ ounces light rum

Soda water

1 lime slice

Combine 4 mint leaves, lime juice and sugar in glass; mash with wooden spoon or muddler. Fill glass with ice. Pour rum over ice; top with soda water. Garnish with lime slice and mint sprigs.

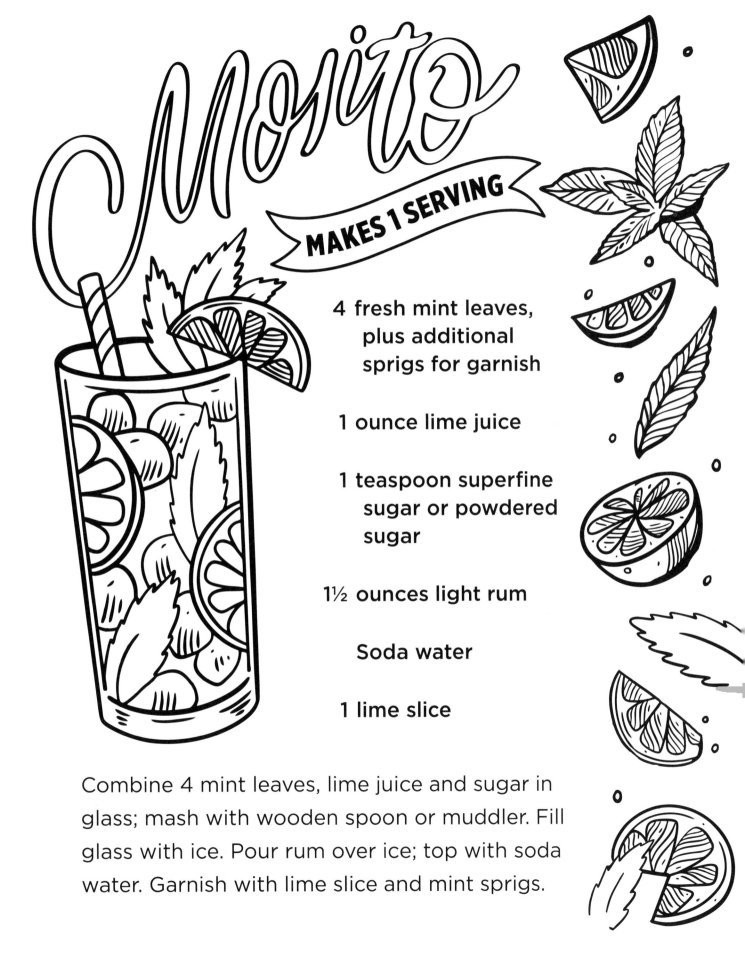

MULLED WINE

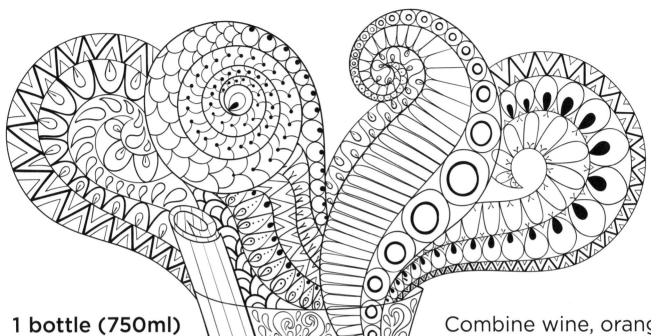

1 bottle (750ml) dry red wine

1 orange, sliced

¼ cup brandy

¼ cup sugar

10 whole cloves

2 cinnamon sticks

2 star anise

Combine wine, orange, brandy, sugar, cloves, cinnamon sticks and star anise in large saucepan; bring to a simmer over medium-low heat. (Keep at about 165°F; do not boil.) Simmer 1 hour; strain before serving. Serve warm.

Makes 6 servings

2 ounces whiskey

1 ounce sweet vermouth

1 dash Angostura bitters

Maraschino cherry

Fill cocktail shaker half full with ice; add whiskey, vermouth and bitters. Stir until blended; strain into cocktail glass or ice-filled old fashioned glass. Garnish with maraschino cherry.

Makes 1 serving

mimosa

4 ounces cold orange juice
4 ounces cold champagne

Orange twist (optional)

Pour orange juice into champagne flute; top with champagne.
Garnish with orange twist.

Makes 1 serving

Bay Breeze

½ cup pineapple juice

1½ ounces vodka

1 ounce cranberry juice

Combine pineapple juice, vodka and cranberry juice in ice-filled glass; stir until well blended.

Makes 1 serving

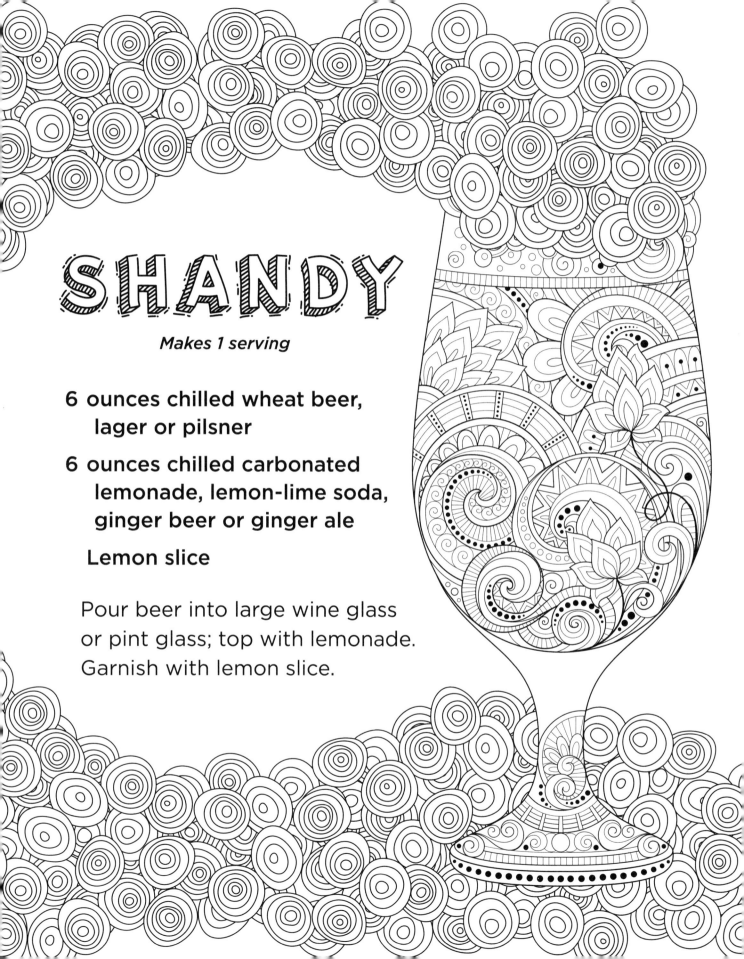

SHANDY

Makes 1 serving

6 ounces chilled wheat beer, lager or pilsner

6 ounces chilled carbonated lemonade, lemon-lime soda, ginger beer or ginger ale

Lemon slice

Pour beer into large wine glass or pint glass; top with lemonade. Garnish with lemon slice.

RUM SWIZZLE

2 ounces rum

1 ounce lime juice

1 teaspoon superfine sugar

2 dashes Angostura bitters

Combine rum, lime juice, sugar and bitters in an ice-filled highball glass; stir vigorously with long spoon until blended.

Makes 1 serving

Piña Colada

4 ounces pineapple juice

1½ ounces light rum

1½ ounces coconut cream

½ cup crushed ice

Pineapple wedge and maraschino cherry

Combine pineapple juice, rum and coconut cream in blender. Add ice; blend 15 seconds or until smooth. Pour into glass; garnish with pineapple and maraschino cherry.

Makes 1 serving

Cosmopolitan

Makes 1 serving

2 ounces vodka or lemon-flavored vodka

1 ounce orange-flavored liqueur

1 ounce cranberry juice

½ ounce lime juice

Lime slice

Fill cocktail shaker half full with ice; add vodka, liqueur, cranberry juice and lime juice. Shake until blended; strain into cocktail glass. Garnish with lime slice.

BUBBLING RASPBERRY COOLERS

¾ cup raspberry vinegar

½ cup sugar

2 liters seltzer water

2 cups fresh raspberries

8 ounces vodka or gin

Fresh mint leaves

1. Bring raspberry vinegar and sugar to a boil in small saucepan over medium heat. Boil 1 minute or until sugar is dissolved, stirring frequently. Cool completely.

2. Pour cooled syrup into large pitcher; stir in seltzer water. To serve, fill each glass with ice, ¼ cup raspberries, 1 ounce vodka and mint leaves. Top with seltzer mixture.

Makes 8 servings

Negroni

1 OUNCE GIN

1 OUNCE CAMPARI

1 OUNCE VERMOUTH

ORANGE PEEL

Fill cocktail shaker half full with ice; add gin, Campari and vermouth. Stir until blended; strain into glass. Garnish with orange peel.

Makes 1 serving

STRAWBERRY BASIL SPARKLERS

1 cup fresh basil leaves

⅔ cup sugar

⅔ cup water

4 cups stemmed fresh strawberries

8 ounces vodka

2 liters club soda

1. Cook basil, sugar and water in small saucepan over medium heat until sugar is dissolved. Remove from heat; cool completely. Pour through fine-mesh sieve; discard basil.

2. Combine strawberries and basil syrup in blender; blend until smooth.

3. Fill eight glasses with ice. Divide strawberry mixture among glasses; pour 1 ounce vodka into each glass. Top with club soda.

Makes 8 servings

Classic Margarita

Lime wedges	4 ounces tequila
Coarse salt	2 ounces triple sec
Ice	2 ounces lime or lemon juice
	Additional lime wedges

1. Rub rim of glasses with lime wedges; dip in salt.

2. Fill cocktail shaker with ice; add tequila, triple sec and lime juice. Shake until blended; strain into glasses. Garnish with additional lime wedges.

Makes 2 servings

HOT TODDY

2 ounces bourbon

1 tablespoon honey

2 teaspoons lemon juice

3/4 cup hot water

cinnamon stick   **lemon slice**

Combine bourbon, honey and lemon juice in mug. Add hot water; stir until blended. Serve with cinnamon stick and lemon slice.

Makes 1 serving

BLOODY MARY

Dash *each* Worcestershire sauce, hot pepper sauce, celery salt, black pepper and salt

3 ounces tomato juice

1½ ounces vodka

½ ounce lemon juice

Celery stalk with leaves, pickle spear, lemon slice and/or green olives

Fill highball glass with ice; add dashes of Worcestershire sauce, hot pepper sauce, celery salt, black pepper and salt. Add tomato juice, vodka and lemon juice; stir gently until blended. Serve with desired garnishes.

Makes 1 serving

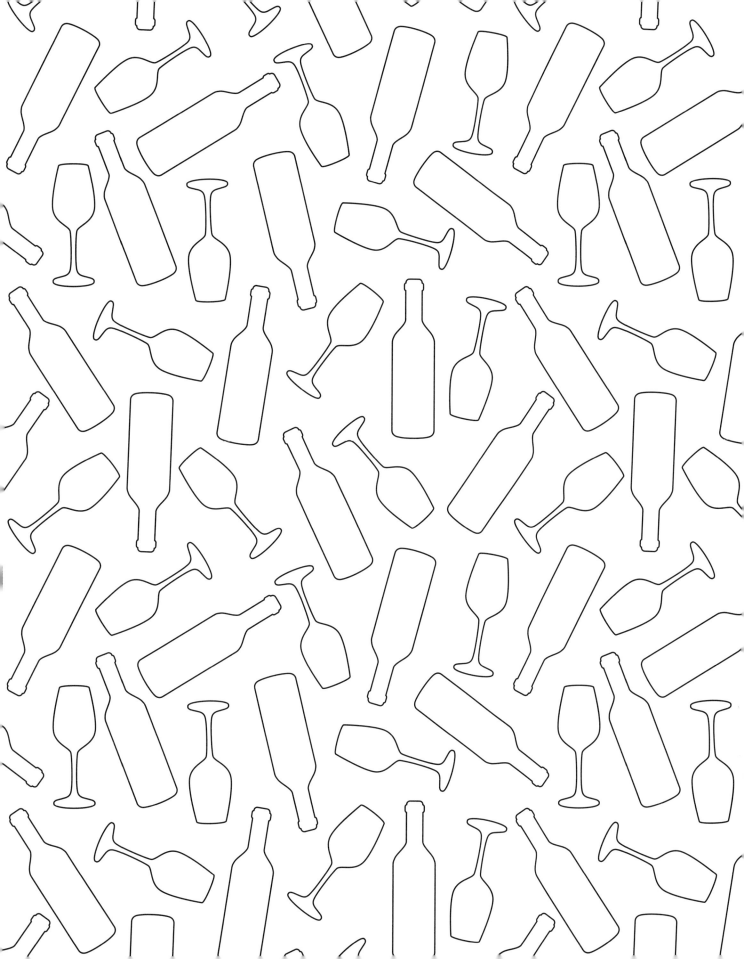